Sports Illustrated KIDS

MORE THAN A GAME

TEAMWORK
ON THE SOCCER FIELD

AND OTHER
SOCCER SKILLS

by Matt Scheff

CAPSTONE PRESS
a capstone imprint

T0011585

Published by Capstone Captivate, an imprint of Capstone.
1710 Roe Crest Drive
North Mankato, Minnesota 56003
capstonepub.com

Library of Congress Cataloging-in-Publication Data
Names: Scheff, Matt, author.
Title: Teamwork on the soccer field : and other soccer skills / by Matt Scheff.
Description: North Mankato, Minnesota : Capstone Captivate is published by Capstone Press, [2022]
| Series: Sports Illustrated Kids: More than a game | Includes bibliographical references and index. |
Audience: Ages 8–11 years | Audience: Grades 4–6 | Summary: "Winning is fun, but it takes more than winning to be a real superstar. Today's soccer superstars know it takes talent, skill, and teamwork on and off the field. This Sports Illustrated Kids title combines fast-paced action, famous plays, and SEL skills to show what sets your favorite athletes and teams apart."—Provided by publisher.
Identifiers: LCCN 2021002885 (print) | LCCN 2021002886 (ebook) | ISBN 9781663906793 (Hardcover) |
ISBN 9781663920737 (Paperback) | ISBN 9781663906762 (PDF) | ISBN 9781663906786 (Kindle Edition)
Subjects: LCSH: Soccer—Juvenile literature. | Soccer—Training—Juvenile literature. | Soccer for children—Juvenile literature.
Classification: LCC GV943.25 .S35 2021 (print) | LCC GV943.25 (ebook) | DDC 796.334—dc23
LC record available at https://lccn.loc.gov/2021002885
LC ebook record available at https://lccn.loc.gov/2021002886

Image Credits
Alamy: PA Images, 11; Associated Press: Dean Mouhtaropoulos, 24; Getty Images: Gareth Copley/Staff, 29, Gary M. Prior/Staff, 13, Mike Hewitt/Staff, 7, MOHAMMED MAHJOUB/Stringer, 14, 15, sampics/Contributor, 21; iStockphoto: PeopleImages, Cover, (right top), skynesher, Cover, (right bottom); Newscom: AFLO/Maurizio Borsari, 28, Bennett Cohen/ZUMA Press, Cover, 4, EFE/Javiar Lizon, 22, Icon SportswireDHZ/Brian Rotmuller, 9, picture-alliance/dpa/Marius Becker, 17, Reuters/MUHAMMAD HAMED, 19, ZUMA Press/Jed Leicester, 23, ZUMA Press/Matthew impey, 10; Shutterstock: Avector, (dots) design element, Hafiz Johari, 6, irin-k (soccer ball) design element, Jacob Lund, Cover, (right middle), Jose Breton- Pics Action, 8, S_Photo (pitch) design element; Sports Illustrated: Al Tielemans, 27, Simon Bruty, 26

Editorial Credits
Editor: Alison Deering; Designer: Heidi Thompson; Media Researcher: Morgan Walters;
Production Specialist: Tori Abraham

All internet sites appearing in back matter were available and accurate when this book was sent to press.

TABLE OF CONTENTS

Glossary terms are **BOLD** on first use.

TEAMWORK, CHARACTER, AND RESPECT

Soccer is the world's most popular sport. Fans love watching their favorite players thread passes and blast shots on goal. But sometimes, soccer is about more than just scoring goals. It's about fair play, compassion, and setting an example for others.

France's Sarah Bouhaddi (left) lends a hand to Alex Morgan (right) of the U.S. women's national team.

Players come together during a match.

Sportsmanship, character, and respect on the field tell a lot about a player or a team. Players help each other up after a fall. They congratulate each other after a great play. They exchange jerseys after matches. And they offer support to both teammates and opponents.

How players act and behave on and off the field is just as important as wins and statistics. It's all about doing the right thing and setting an example for all to follow.

SETTING AN EXAMPLE

In big-time soccer, winning is a big deal. But for many teams and players, it's about more than that. It's also about fair play.

Looking Out for an Opponent

In December 2000, Everton and West Ham United, two clubs in the English Premier League (EPL), were locked in a 1–1 tie. Late in the match, Everton's goalkeeper, Paul Gerrard, hurt his knee as he moved to defend a West Ham rush. Play continued as Gerrard lie on the ground. He was in pain.

West Ham forward Paolo Di Canio took a pass near the goal. It was a chance for an easy goal in a tie game. It could have been West Ham's chance to take the lead.

But Di Canio didn't take the shot. Instead, he caught the pass. That caused play to stop so that Gerrard could get medical help. It was a show of **empathy** and compassion for a fellow player and a true display of sportsmanship.

West Ham's Paolo Di Canio (right) receives a special award for sportsmanship from Paul Gerrard (left) of Everton.

Showing the Way

When it comes to teamwork, it's hard to top the 2019 United States women's national team (USWNT). The U.S. dominated the Women's World Cup. They used **precision** passing, electric goal-scoring, and firm defense to win all of their games on the way to the title.

The popularity of women's soccer had been on the rise for decades. But the amazing teamwork of the 2019 team took it to a new level. They set an example for young athletes everywhere. They showed that with teamwork, anything is possible.

The USWNT celebrated after winning the final match of the FIFA Women's World Cup in 2019.

Fans supported the ongoing fight for equal pay during the USA Victory Tour match between the U.S. and the Republic of Ireland in 2019.

USWNT players also fought for equal pay with men, who earned far more money for playing on the national team. It was a demand for respect that was hard to ignore.

Clive Clarke goes after the ball during a match.

Fair Play

In 2007, Leicester and Nottingham Forest faced off in a match. Nottingham took control in the first half. They led 1–0 at the break. But during halftime, Leicester's Clive Clarke collapsed in the locker room. It was a heart attack—a serious medical problem. The game was called off.

Thankfully, Clarke survived. The game was replayed a few weeks later. By rule, it started over at 0–0. But Leicester knew that Nottingham had earned a lead. They made the surprising decision to let Nottingham score a goal to start the game. That reset the score to 1–0.

In a game where teams go all out to win, Leicester showed that sometimes fairness was more important.

Nottingham Forest's manager, Colin Calderwood, speaks to the crowd.

Getting It Right

The stakes were high when Liverpool and Arsenal faced off in 1997. Winning was important to Liverpool's Robbie Fowler. But he wanted to do it the right way. When Fowler fell near the Arsenal goal, an official called a foul on the goalkeeper.

Fowler knew that he hadn't been tripped. He'd just fallen. He told the official, but the foul stood. Fowler was awarded a penalty kick, but the kick was weak. It looked like Fowler hadn't even tried to score.

Fowler denied that he'd missed on purpose, but the truth was clear to anyone watching. Fowler hadn't wanted to score on the kick. His act of sportsmanship didn't cost his team. Liverpool won the match 2–1. And they did it without the benefit of a bad call.

The Jersey Exchange

Exchanging jerseys after a match is a soccer tradition. In a show of sportsmanship and respect, players often meet at midfield to talk and swap jerseys. It's a way to connect with opponents in a warm and friendly way. Many soccer stars treasure their collections of opponent's jerseys.

Tony Adams (left) of Arsenal grabs the jersey of Liverpool's Robbie Fowler (right).

Tied Up

In November 2013, Al-Nahda and Al-Ittihad were locked in a tight 2–2 Saudi Premier League match. After taking a pass, Al-Nahda's goalkeeper Taisir Al Antaif realized that his shoe was untied. Goalkeepers wear large gloves, meaning Al Antaif would be unable to tie his own shoe.

Al-Ittihad's Mohammed Ali (left) chases Yousif Mahammed (right) of Al-Nahda during a match.

Majid Salim (left) of Al-Nahda and Akram Abbad (right) of Al-Ittihad fight for the control of the ball.

Al-Ittihad striker Jobson noticed the problem. He ran over and tied Al Antaif's shoe for him. An official thought the goalkeeper was wasting time, however, and called a foul.

Al-Ittihad had no interest in cashing in. They booted the ball out of bounds on the free kick. The game was reset, and play continued, eventually ending in a 4–4 tie. It was a show of empathy and sportsmanship that gained worldwide attention.

SHOWING SUPPORT

Soccer can be a hard game. Sometimes it takes the support of teammates—or opponents—to get through a tough time. Whether it's personal tragedy or just a bad day, a show of support can make all the difference.

Paying Tribute

Winger James Rodríguez was a superstar for Colombia's national team in the 2014 World Cup. He scored six goals in the tournament and carried his team. Still, Colombia was no match for Brazil in the quarter-finals. They were defeated 2–1.

Rodríguez was emotional as the final minutes ticked away. All his hard work hadn't been enough. Brazil's David Luiz saw his opponent's pain. He approached Rodríguez and waved toward the crowd telling them to cheer.

The crowd did just that. They rose to their feet and gave Rodríguez a huge **ovation**. Luiz's show of empathy didn't take away the sting of losing. But it helped Rodríguez walk off the field a winner in his own way.

Brazil's David Luiz (left) comforted opponent, James Rodríguez (right) of Colombia, following a 2014 FIFA World Cup game.

Building a Wall

The game isn't always the biggest thing on the line in soccer. That was true when Shabab al Ordon Club faced Arab Orthodox Club (AOC) in the 2017 West Asian Football Federation Women's Championship.

During the match, an AOC player realized that her **hijab** was slipping off her head. In the Islamic faith, a hijab is an important head covering for a woman. It's part of the culture for a woman to cover her head and hair. Having it fall off would have been embarrassing or even shameful.

The AOC player slowed as she tried to fix the hijab. Shabab's players saw what was happening and understood. Instead of continuing play, they formed a human wall, providing their opponent privacy as she fixed the hijab. Their show of empathy and compassion became a **social media** sensation.

Women's Soccer in the Arab World

Many people in the Arab world have strict ideas about women. For years, women were banned from public sports. In some countries, they couldn't even attend matches! But that has changed in recent decades. Muslim countries such as Turkey and Jordan now allow women to play sports—including soccer.

Shabab al Ordon players warm up before a match in Amman, Jordan.

Reaching Out

Bayern Munich and Valencia were locked in a tight battle in the UEFA Champions League 2000-2001. It was a matchup between great goalkeepers. Santiago Canizares was a star for Valencia. Bayern Munich's Oliver Kahn was famous for his great skill—and his big heart. Both were on display in the final moments of the big match.

The game was tied 1–1 after extra time. That meant penalty kicks would decide the winner. Kahn made a huge save and clinched the game for Bayern. Canizares dropped to the ground in disappointment as Bayern rushed the field.

The Fair Play Code

FIFA, the organizing body for international soccer, has a Fair Play Code that it expects players to honor. The code includes ten rules of fair play.

1. Play to win.
2. Accept defeat with dignity.
3. Observe the laws of the game.
4. Respect opponents, teammates, referees, officials, and spectators.
5. Promote the interests of soccer.
6. Honor those who defend soccer's good reputation.
7. Reject corruption, drugs, racism, violence, gambling, and dangers to the sport.
8. Help others reject corruption.
9. Speak out against those who cheat.
10. Use soccer to make a better world.

But Kahn didn't join in. Instead, he rushed over to Canizares. It was an inspiring act of compassion and sportsmanship. It was more important to Kahn to show concern for a friend and competitor than it was to celebrate.

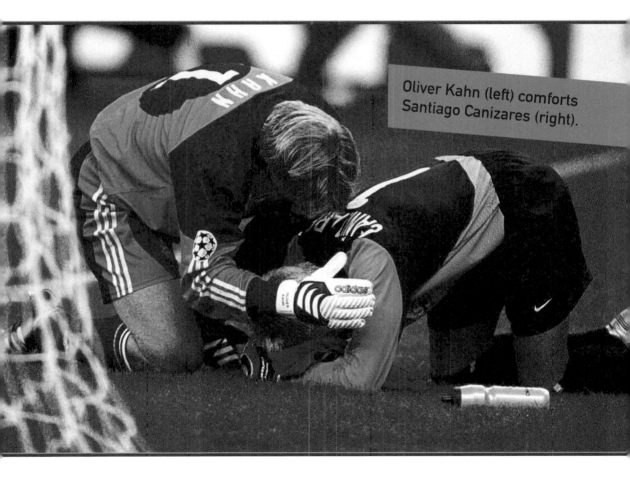

Oliver Kahn (left) comforts Santiago Canizares (right).

A Show of Support

Real Madrid is Barcelona's biggest **rival**. But that didn't stop the team from showing its support for their competition during a difficult time. In 2012, Barcelona's Eric Abidal was going through a health crisis. He needed an emergency liver **transplant**. It was a big deal, and no one knew how it would turn out.

Real Madrid players wear T-shirts in support of Barcelona's defender Eric Abidal.

In a show of support, Real Madrid players wore T-shirts that read *Animo Abidal* or *Soul Abidal* before a March 2012 match. Other shirts said *Get well soon Muamba*. That was for Fabrice Muamba, a player from the Bolton Wanderers. Muamba had collapsed on the field the day before due to a heart attack.

The Real Madrid players were showing empathy for two fellow players going through tough times. They proved compassion can come before competition.

West Ham United's Kevin Nolan (left) and Carlton Cole (right) wear T-shirts for Barcelona's Eric Abidal and Bolton's Fabrice Muamba.

MORE THAN A GAME

Sometimes soccer is bigger than just the match. It's about social and global issues. It's a chance for teams and players to lead and set an example.

Players from the USWNT wore *Black Lives Matter* shirts ahead of a game against the Netherlands in November 2020.

Standing Up

In 2020, **social justice** was on the minds of many players. Following the deaths of George Floyd, Breonna Taylor, and other Black men and women in the United States, members of the National Women's Soccer League wanted to speak out. They wanted to lead.

The U.S. women's national team wore shirts with the words *Black Lives Matter* on them before their first game of the Challenge Cup in June 2020. It was a slogan representing the fight for social justice. In November 2020, they wore *Black Lives Matter* warm-up jackets ahead of their game against the Netherlands.

Many players also posted a joint statement on their social media accounts. "We love our country, and it is a true honor to represent America. It is also our duty to demand that the liberties and freedoms that our country was founded on extend to everyone."

Peace over Politics

Tension between the United States and Iran were high when the two met at the 1998 World Cup. Violence had broken out between the two nations. No one was sure what to expect at the match. The host country, France, feared that the tension could boil over. French officials had extra security at the match.

But there was no reason to worry. The U.S. and Iranian players proved that peace was the better way. The players from Iran gifted their American opponents with white roses before the match. White roses are a symbol of peace. Then the players all gathered to pose for photographs.

Iran ultimately came out on top, 2–1. But in this match, everyone left a winner.

Players from the United States and Iran posed together at the 1998 World Cup.

Frankie Hejduk (left) of the United States and Iran's Mehrdad Minavand (right) in action during the 1998 World Cup.

Acting Fast

Soccer players have to think and act quickly. But that took on a new meaning in a March 2014 match between Dynamo Kiev and Dnipro. Dynamo Kiev's captain, Oleg Gusev, collapsed on the field after a collision with another player. Gusev had swallowed his own tongue. He was choking.

Dnipro midfielder Jaba Kankava rushed to Gusev's side. He stuck his hand down Gusev's throat to clear his airway. Sports aren't usually life-or-death. But this time it was Kankava's quick action that probably saved his opponent's life.

Dnipro midfielder Jaba Kankava

Dynamo Kiev's captain, Oleg Gusev, in action in 2015.

Kankava was a hero. He showed that teamwork didn't just extend to players wearing the same jerseys. It's about looking out for everyone—teammates and opponents alike—and using soccer as a way to lead and set an example that anyone can follow.

GLOSSARY

empathy (EM-puh-thee)—imagining how others feel

hijab (hi-JAHB)—a traditional covering for the hair and neck that is worn by Muslim women

ovation (oh-VEY-shuhn)—an expression of approval or enthusiasm made by clapping or cheering

precision (prih-SI-zhun)—with exact accuracy

rival (RYE-vuhl)—a person or team with whom one has an especially intense competition

social justice (SOH-shuhl JUHSS-tiss)—equality and fairness for all people in a society

social media (SOH-shuhl MEE-dee-uh)—forms of electronic communication, such as websites, through which people create online communities to share information, ideas, and personal messages

transplant (TRANSS-plant)—an operation in which a diseased organ is replaced with a healthy one

READ MORE

Kortemeier, Todd. *Fairness in Sports*. Lake Elmo, MN: Focus Readers, 2018.

Robinson, David. *The Ultimate Game: Life Lessons From Sports*. Nampa, Idaho: Pacific Press Publishing Association, 2019.

INTERNET SITES

Inspiring Acts of Sportsmanship That Show Off the Best of Humanity
esquiremag.ph/life/sports/inspiring-acts-of-sportsmanship-that-show-off-the-best-of-sports-a1729-20180704-lfrm

SIKids: Soccer
sikids.com/tag/soccer

10 Basics of Sportsmanship for Kids
verywellfamily.com/basic-sportsmanship-for-kids-1257031

INDEX